The Safe Christmas Cookbook

Contents

Introduction

Simple Steps to Safe Christmas Cooking

HACCP

A Brief Guide to the Food Safety Jargon Used in this Book

Cool Rules for a Cool Christmas

Allergy and Food Intolerance

Accompaniments

Sweet Chestnut Stuffing
Brandy Butter
Sage and Onion Stuffing
Traditional Bread Sauce
Cranberry Sauce
Turkey Giblet Stock
Gravy
Yorkshire Puddings
Roasted Vegetables

Starters

Turkey Pate
Turkey Soup
Leek and Potato Soup
Tuna Stuffed Tomatoes
Potted Christmas Stilton
Prawn Cocktail

Main Courses

Lentil Roast
Traditional Roast Turkey
Baked Sugar Glazed Gammon
Courgette Terrine
Unstuffed Roast Goose
Honey Roast Pheasant

Desserts

Traditional Christmas Pudding
Soured Cream Cheesecake
Traditional Sherry Trifle
Chocolate Orange Trifle
Chocolate Bread Pudding
Figgy Pudding

Nibbles

Sausage Rolls
Hazelnut Cakes
Rich Shortbread
Chocolate Truffles
Mince pies

Weights and Measures

Notes

Introduction

Christmas comes but once a year and when it does it brings good cheer.... and, sometimes, sickness and diarrhoea and turkey bones stuck in the throat. Yes, Christmas is a wonderful time but it is also a time when people expose themselves to the rigours of cooking more food at one go and feeding more people in one sitting than at any other time of the year. It is hardly surprising then, that the festive season is also a peak time for food related illness.

The Food Standards Agency report, published in October of 2002, estimated there to be over a million cases of food related illness in the UK over the course of a year and a lack of the application of even basic food safety principles in many commercial kitchens. What they didn't mention was that the majority of food poisoning is reported by individuals and families and very often can be tracked back to unsafe things being done to food in the home.

The causes vary but examples include:
- putting raw meat above open cheese in a fridge
- using the same things to work with raw vegetables and cooked meat
- leaving the shopping in the car for a couple of hours, all mixed up in the shopping bags, raw and cooked, meat and salad
- not washing hands before handling food or after going to the loo or stroking the dog...

Well, we at Achor Partners thought it was especially a shame for people to get sick at Christmas. It seems a pity for you to have to celebrate Jesus' birthday locked in the loo and missing out on all that Christmas pud and chocolate treats. So we thought, a little helpful advice wrapped around some of the most delicious Christmas recipes we could find would help. Above all cooking at Christmas should be fun. So, have the confidence to have a go, but safely.

Have a very merry and healthy Christmas!

From the Achor team.

Simple Steps to Safe Christmas Cooking

1. Always wash your hands thoroughly, paying particular attention to fingertips and nails:
    - Before preparing or eating food
    - After preparing meat or raw vegetables
    - After using the lavatory.

2. Ensure all work surfaces and utensils are clean and have been sterilised by scalding with very hot water or sprayed with a food safe sanitiser to reduce bacteria.

3. Ensure that **no** surfaces or utensils used for raw meat or raw vegetables come into contact with food that has been cooked or is to be eaten without cooking.

4. Keep food either very cold (below 10°C) or very hot (above 63°C) and always keep it covered.

Note: the 'use within' storage times given for the recipes in this book assume that the food WILL BE REFRIGERATED or stored in an air tight container as appropriate.

5. Wear a clean full apron while you are cooking and keep your hair tied out of the way. This will not only protect you and your clothes but will protect the food you are preparing from loose hairs and anything harmful on you.

6. Remove all jewellery except plain gold rings and cover any cuts, spots or other skin damage, with a waterproof dressing.

7. Keep pets as far away from food as possible (except their own!).

8. Check all dry ingredients for 'foreign bodies'. That is **anything** that shouldn't be there, such as creepy crawlies, bits of packaging etc. It is a good idea to sieve flour and other fine powders into the mixing bowl to avoid lumps and allow a visual check at the same time.

9. Check use by dates on ingredient packs, especially important on little used ingredients.

10. Check packaging for damage and tins for dents and ensure all seals are unbroken. If in doubt do not use.

HACCP

The food safety advice for each recipe has been worked out carefully using a system known as HACCP. This stands for Hazard Analysis and Critical Control Point. It is a process used commercially to identify where things can go wrong in food preparation potentially leading to illness. Monitoring these points and working out actions to prevent the hazard can prevent someone becoming ill.

A Brief Guide to the Food Safety Jargon Used in this Book

Hazard
A potential happening, which could cause illness or injury.

Control Point
A point in a process of food preparation at which the risk of the hazard becoming a reality (reaching an unacceptable level of risk for the consumer), may be controlled.

Critical Control Point
A point in a process at which the risk from a serious hazard can and must be effectively controlled, thus preventing the risk to the consumer of the food becoming unacceptable. Proper control action at this point will very substantially reduce the risk of illness or injury for the consumer of the food.

Hygiene
Hygiene is the process of safe food by taking all reasonable and practicable steps to prevent anything getting into the food that shouldn't be there.

Bacteria
Microscopic creatures that are present everywhere, especially in soil and on animals (including us). Some of them, along with some viruses (even smaller) and some fungi are 'pathogens' and can cause illness.

Mould
Tiny, furry fungi that cause off flavours in food and in a few cases, produce dangerous poisons (toxins) that leak into the food.

Foreign body
Anything found contaminating the food that shouldn't be there – the most often found foreign bodies in food are hairs.

Cool Rules for a Cool Christmas

We use freezers and fridges all the time. Cooling the food down seriously hampers the reproductive life of bacteria. However if these cooling machines are not treated with caution and respect and used to clear rules then disaster can follow.

Cool rules

Cover anything that you put in a fridge or freezer.

Put raw meat and any uncooked vegetables at the bottom of the fridge.

Put dairy products and things that will not be heated again on upper shelves of the fridge.

Check the temperature at each level in your fridge or freezer. Fridges should be between 2°C and 7°C and freezers should be between -18°C and - 22°C.

Re-heat food thoroughly you have stored in the fridge that you intend to eat hot so that it is **very hot** throughout.

DO NOT put hot food straight into the fridge or freezer, let it cool to room temperature first for at most 90 minutes.

DO NOT refreeze food once it has been thawed.

DO NOT overcrowd your fridge or freezer - air must be able to flow freely around the food in order that it can cool properly.

Allergy and Food Intolerance

Although sometimes it seems some people are merely faddy and there are a lot of strange diets around some folk genuinely and potentially dangerously react to certain foods. Common substances include nuts, fish products—especially sea food such as prawns, dairy products and egg protein. Moulds especially in the form of airborne spores may also affect some people.

Allergic symptoms range from a minor rash through swelling and distortion of surface tissues to respiratory distress and complete circulatory collapse and death within 30 minutes of exposure. This last effect is fortunately very rare.

Those who are intolerant to certain food stuffs may be violently sick, develop headaches or have diarrhoea. Some may show symptoms of both allergy and intolerance.

To make sure you don't inadvertently ruin someone's (and your own) Christmas here are some simple rules to follow:

- Take care when preparing dishes containing nuts, fish or cheese that there is no cross contamination between utensils / hands / surfaces onto other ingredients or dishes not containing these.
- Avoid using peanuts (ground nuts) or peanut oil (ground nut oil) or fillers such as ground almonds unless you are **CERTAIN** none of your guests has a nut allergy. Only a trace of peanuts can be fatal to an unfortunate few.
- Check with your guests for any serious allergies or intolerances **BEFORE** serving at a sit down / formal meal and ensure you know what is in soups, puddings etc. It is embarrassing to have to ask when the portion is in front of you. And ensure you have a simple alternative available such as fresh fruit.
- For a buffet when little known guests may be mingling avoid nuts used merely as decoration if the rest of the dish does not contain nuts.
- Ensure any seafood or fish is clearly visible and obvious.
- Do not put unexpected ingredients into traditional dishes such as cream cheese in mince pies.

Finally don't panic but do take allergy and intolerance problems seriously and ensure all your guests feel welcome and included in the celebration.

Sweet Chestnut Stuffing

Ingredients

2 slices of dry bread, crumbled
1 small onion
1 egg
225g (8oz) sweet chestnuts,
shelled (or puree)

1 teaspoon dried parsley
1 teaspoon dried thyme
1 teaspoon dried sage
1 teaspoon (5ml) lemon juice

Cooking
Oven proof dish or baking tray

Method
1. Bring a pan of water to the boil and drop in the chestnuts to remove the skins.
2. Place in a bowl and mash (omit these steps if using puree).
3. Add all the remaining ingredients and mix thoroughly.
4. Use immediately to stuff turkey OR
5. Place in an ovenproof dish or on a baking tray in separate 'dollops' and bake for ¼ hour at 160°C, 325°F, gas mark 3.

Hazards
Bacterial contamination of the chestnut puree and egg.

Critical Control Points
Step 2
If using ready made puree make sure it is taken fresh from an unopened can or from a source that has been pasteurised. Do not keep any un-used puree or make your own ahead of beginning this recipe.
Step 4, 5
Ensure mixture is piping hot all the way through when cooked.

Use within - 5 days

Brandy Butter

─Ingredients─

115g (4oz) butter, softened
115g (4oz) icing sugar, sifted
115g (4oz) castor sugar
1 tablespoon (15ml) fresh milk
1 tablespoon (15ml) brandy

55g (2oz) ground almonds

Method

1. Beat butter in a small mixing bowl until creamy.
2. Gradually beat in icing sugar, castor sugar, milk and brandy.
3. Cream together until light and fluffy.
4. Add the ground almonds and mix well.
5. Use fresh within 6 hours with hot mince pies or Christmas pudding.
6. Refrigerate in a closed container for later use.

Hazards

Hypersensitivity to nuts in some people, if in doubt omit from recipe.

Use within - 3 days

Sage and Onion Stuffing with Pork Sausage Meat

Ingredients

900g (2lb) pork sausage meat
4 tablespoons breadcrumbs
1 tablespoon dried sage

1 large onion, finely chopped
1 egg, beaten with a little water
Salt and pepper to season

Method
1. Mix the breadcrumbs, onion and sage together in a large bowl.
2. Add the sausage meat and beaten egg.
3. Season with salt and pepper and stir well until thoroughly mixed.
4. Use immediately to stuff the turkey or store covered in the fridge until required.

Hazards
Bacteria from hands, egg and sausage meat.
Cross contamination from the raw
sausage meat.

Critical Control Points
Wash hands thoroughly before and after handling the raw sausage meat.
Wash utensils and storage containers thoroughly after use in very hot water.

Use within - 24 hours

Traditional Bread Sauce

Ingredients - Serves 8

115g (4oz) fresh breadcrumbs
1 large onion
16 whole cloves
1 bay leaf
8 black peppercorns

600ml (1 pint) full cream milk
55g (2oz) butter
2 tablespoons (30ml) double cream
Salt and black pepper to season

Method

1. Cut the onion in half and push in the cloves all over. Place the onion, bayleaf and the peppercorns in a saucepan.
2. Add the milk, sprinkle in a little salt and bring to the boil.
3. Remove from the heat and cover the pan. Leave in a warm place for the milk to infuse for 2 hours.
4. Remove the bay leaf, onion and peppercorns.
5. Stir the breadcrumbs into the milk and add half the butter.
6. Put the saucepan on a very low heat, stirring occasionally for about 15 minutes until the crumbs have swollen and the sauce has thickened. Gently beat in the rest of the butter and cream. Season with salt and pepper to taste.

Hazards

Bacteria in the milk.

Critical Control Points

Step 2
Bring the milk to the boil for 1 minute.
Step 6
Maintain the mixture close to boiling throughout the simmering period.

Use within - 3 days

Cranberry Sauce

Ingredients

300ml (½ pint) water
175g (6oz) granulated sugar
225g (8oz) of cranberries, washed

Method

1. Place sugar in a pan with the water and heat gently until the sugar has dissolved.
2. Add the cranberries, bring to the boil and boil quickly until the skins split open (about 2-3 minutes).
3. Reduce the heat and simmer for a further 10 minutes.
4. Either serve immediately hot or cool slowly and store in the fridge in an airtight container until required. Can be served hot or cold to accompany hot or cold meats.

Hazards

Surface fungi and bacteria on the cranberries.

Critical Control Points

Step 2
Ensure mixture boils (continuous bubbling that cannot be 'stirred out').
Step 3
Ensure a syrupy gel forms as the mixture simmers.

Use within - 5 days

Turkey Giblet Stock

Ingredients

Turkey giblets, including neck	1 bay leaf
1 onion	A sprig of parsley
1 medium carrot	Salt and black pepper to season
1 celery stalk	900ml (1½ pints) water

Method

1. Wash the giblets and place in a pan with the water.
2. Cut the onion and carrot in half lengthways and add to the pan.
3. Bring to the boil and remove any scum that rises to the surface with a slotted spoon.
4. Add the remaining ingredients and cover the pan with a lid.
5. Simmer for 1½ - 2 hours. Strain and allow to cool for a maximum of 90 minutes then store in the fridge until required.

Hazards

Bacteria from giblets and hands.

Critical Control Points

Step 3
Ensure the stock boils for at least 1 minute.
Step 5
Ensure that the simmering temperature is close to boiling throughout.

Use within - 3 days (Re-boil for 3 minutes before use)

Gravy

Ingredients

Meat juices from the roasting tin	300ml (½ pint) stock
1 tablespoon (15g) cornflour	(from a stock cube or vegetable water)

Method

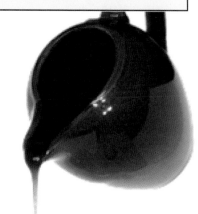

1. Separate most of the fat from the juices and discard. (The fat will float and can be gently spooned off from the top).
2. Pour the juices into a saucepan. Gradually add the cornflour, stirring continuously to ensure a smooth mix.
3. Using a low heat gradually blend in the stock or vegetable water.
4. Bring to the boil stirring constantly until the gravy thickens.
5. Lower the heat and simmer gently for 3 minutes.

Hazards

Bacteria from ingredients and utensils.

Critical Control Points

Step 5

Ensure gravy has reached a full boiling point before simmering.

Note – if any is kept, cover while it cools for up to 90 minutes and then refrigerate immediately below 10°C. Ensure that it is brought back up to boiling point for at least three minutes before reuse.

Use within - 2 days

Yorkshire Pudding

Ingredients - Makes 12

115g (4oz) plain flour
1 egg
300ml (½ pint) fresh milk

25g (1oz) oil or margarine
Pinch of salt

Cooking
12 hole bun tin

Method
1. Sieve the flour and salt together in a bowl.
2. Break the egg and gradually add the milk, beating until smooth with a fork, whisk or electric mixer.
3. Pre heat the oven to 220° C, 450° F or gas mark 6.
4. Grease the tin with the oil or margarine and place in the oven for 1 minute or until melted.
5. Gently pour in the batter and cook in the top of the oven for 15 to 20 minutes until golden brown and crispy.

Hazards
Bacteria in the egg.

Critical Control Points
Bake puddings until 'piping' hot throughout.

Use within - 24 hours

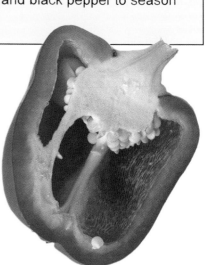

Roasted Vegetables

Ingredients - Serves 4

3 courgettes, sliced lengthways
3 medium carrots, sliced lengthways
4 small onions, halved
2 red peppers cut into thick slices
115g (4oz) button mushrooms

½ medium swede, cut into small chunks
3 tablespoons (45ml) olive oil
Salt and black pepper to season

Cooking
Baking tray

Method
1. Mix all the vegetables in a large bowl and toss in olive oil until well coated.
2. Pre heat the oven to 220°C, 450°F or gas mark 6.
3. Place vegetables on a baking tray, season with salt and pepper and roast for 45 minutes or until all the vegetables are tender and slightly blackened around the edges.

Hazards
Bacteria from hands.
Foreign bodies, bacteria on vegetables.

Critical Control Points
Wash hands thoroughly before starting. Wash all vegetables thoroughly.

Use within - 2 days

Turkey Pate

Ingredients

115g (4oz) butter
225g (8oz) cooked turkey, minced
1 tablespoon (15ml) sherry
½ teaspoon lemon juice
2 or 3 drops of Tabasco or
Worcester Sauce
Pinch ground cloves
Salt and pepper to taste

55g (2oz) butter, melted

Cooking
Small individual pots or attractive china dish

Method
1. Cream the butter and mix in the minced turkey.
2. Add the sherry, lemon juice, sauce and cloves and stir well to thoroughly mix the ingredients.
3. Season to taste with the salt and pepper.
4. Put into one china dish or individual pots, smooth the surface and pour over the melted butter.
5. Cover with aluminium foil and chill before serving.

Hazards
Bacteria in the cooked turkey.

Critical Control Points
Step 1
Use meat that has been kept no longer than two days and has been refrigerated below 10°C throughout.
Step 5
After chilling do not keep at room temperature for more than one hour before serving.
Re-chill any that is left over below 10°C immediately.

Use within - 3 days

Turkey Soup

Ingredients - Serves 4

For the stock
1 turkey carcass, including skin, bone and left over meat
1 medium carrot, sliced
1 onion cut in half
1 stick of celery, cut in half
1 teaspoon dried thyme
2 bay leaves

For the soup
450g (1lb) mixed vegetables per 600ml (1 pint) of turkey stock
15g (½oz) butter per 450g (1lb of vegetables)
salt and black pepper to season

Method

1. Make the stock by breaking up the carcass and putting it into a large pan with the rest of the stock ingredients.
2. Cover with water and bring to the boil. Reduce the heat and simmer gently for 2 hours. Remove any scum that rises to the surface with a slotted spoon.
3. Strain the stock and discard the leftovers.
4. Make the soup by putting the chopped vegetables in a large pan and adding the turkey stock.
5. Bring to the boil and simmer for 1½ hours.
6. Puree using a blender or by rubbing through a sieve.
7. Season to taste with the salt and pepper.
8. Return to the saucepan and thoroughly re heat.

Hazards

Bacteria from the turkey carcass and hands.
Bones from the carcass.

Critical Control Points

Step 2, 5
Boil the stock for at least 1 minute, simmer the soup close to boiling.
Step 6
Ensure no bone fragments remain in the soup once pureed.

Use within – 3 days (Reboil for 3 minutes before use.)

Leek and Potato Soup

Ingredients - Serves 4

450g (1lb) potatoes
450g (1lb) leeks
1 onion
55g (2oz) butter
300ml (½ pint) milk

750ml (1¼ pints) chicken stock
(home made or using stock cube)
Salt and pepper for seasoning

Method

1. Peel and dice the potatoes.
2. Clean and trim the leeks.
3. Slice the onion.
4. Melt the butter in a large pan and cook the vegetables for 5 minutes.
5. Add the stock and simmer for 20 minutes.
6. Using a blender, blend until smooth.
7. Add the milk and blend again to ensure thorough mixing.
8. Transfer back to the saucepan and re-heat gently, season to taste.
9. Serve with a garnish of fresh herbs such as parsley and chives.

Hazards

Bacteria from the milk, chicken stock and vegetables.

Critical Control Points

Steps 1 and 2
Wash vegetables thoroughly.
Step 8
Ensure soup simmers close to boiling, re-boil before serving if stored.

Use within - 2 days

Tuna Stuffed Tomatoes

Ingredients - Serves 8

4 very large, firm tomatoes, halved and with the seeds removed
2 hard boiled eggs, finely chopped
200g (7oz) tin of tuna, drained and flaked

1 teaspoon chopped fresh parsley
3 tablespoons (45 ml) mayonnaise
4 stuffed olives, halved for garnish

Method

1. Turn the halved tomatoes upside down onto kitchen paper to drain.
2. Place all the ingredients except the olives in a bowl and mix well.
3. Place the tomatoes the right way up on a serving plate and pile in the mixture evenly. Garnish with the olives.

Hazards

Bacteria on hands and utensils and in mayonnaise and eggs. Sensitivity to fish in some people, especially when the fish is left at room temperature for any length of time.

Critical Control Points

Step 2
Ensure eggs are thoroughly hard boiled.
Step 3
Serve and eat within four hours.

Use within - do not keep

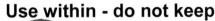

Potted Christmas Stilton

Ingredients

225g (8oz) Stilton cheese
85g (3oz) butter
2 teaspoons (10ml) port
Pinch of ground mace
A little melted butter

Cooking
Small serving dish or attractive jar

Method
1. Mash the stilton with a fork.
2. Beat the butter in a bowl to a soft cream then stir in the stilton, mace and port and beat gently until well mixed and smooth.
3. Pack the mixture into the jar or serving dish and smooth over the surface.
4. Pour the melted butter over the top to act as a seal.
5. Keep in the fridge until required. Serve with fresh bread or crackers.

Hazards
Mould and bacteria on cheese in storage.
Bacteria on hands and packaging.

Critical Control Points
Wash hands thoroughly before preparing the food and ensure all utensils and containers are scalded and clean as the food is not cooked.

Use within - Store below 5°C for up to 10 days

Prawn Cocktail

Ingredients - Serves 4

½ lettuce, washed and dried
2 tablespoons (30ml) mayonnaise
4 tablespoons (60ml) natural yogurt
3 tablespoons (45ml) tomato ketchup
2 tablespoons (30ml) Worcester sauce

2 tablespoons (30ml) creamed horseradish
2 tablespoons (30ml) lemon juice
225g (8oz) peeled prawns
Brown bread and butter to serve

Method
1. Shred lettuce and half fill 4 large wine or dessert glasses.
2. In a bowl mix together the mayonnaise and yogurt, stir in tomato ketchup, Worcester Sauce, horseradish and lemon juice.
3. Add the prawns and mix well.
4. Spoon the mix equally into the 4 glasses.
5. Serve with slices of brown bread and butter.

Hazards
Bacteria in mayonnaise, yougurt and prawns.
Hypersensitive reaction to prawns by some people, especially if prawns are left at room temperature for any length of time.

Critical Control Points
Store below 10°C until ready to serve for no longer than 4 hours, consume immediately.

Use within - do not keep

Main Courses

Lentil Roast

Ingredients - Serves 6

225g (8oz) red lentils
450ml (¾ pint) fresh vegetable stock (vegetable water or a stock cube)
1 bay leaf
15g (½oz) butter or margarine, softened
2 tablespoons dried wholemeal breadcrumbs
225g (8oz) mature cheddar, grated

1 leek, cleaned, trimmed and finely chopped
115g (4oz) mushrooms, finely chopped
85g (3oz) fresh wholemeal breadcrumbs
2 tablespoons (30ml) lemon juice
2 eggs, beaten
Salt and black pepper to season

Cooking
1kg (2lb) loaf tin, baking parchment

Method
1. Put the lentils, stock and bay leaf in a saucepan and bring to the boil.
2. Simmer gently for 15 – 20 minutes until the lentils have absorbed all the liquid and are soft. Discard the bay leaf.
3. Line a 1kg (2lb) loaf tin with baking parchment and grease well. Sprinkle with the dried breadcrumbs.
4. Stir the cheese, leek, mushrooms and fresh breadcrumbs into the lentil mixture.
5. Add the beaten eggs with the lemon juice to bind the mixture together, season with the salt and pepper and spoon into the tin.
6. Bake in a pre heated oven, 200°C, 400°F, gas mark 5 for one hour or until golden.
7. Turn out onto a serving dish and garnish with fresh parsley or other herbs as available.

Hazards
Bacteria in cheese and eggs. Foreign bodies in lentils.

Critical Control Points
Step 1
Visually check lentils before adding to saucepan.
Step 6
Cook until too hot to touch and steaming when removed from the oven.

Use within - 2 days

Traditional Roast Turkey

Ingredients

Minimum 4 - 5Kg (10lb) turkey
115g (4oz) softened butter
8 rashers streaky bacon

Made up stuffing
Salt and pepper to season

Cooking
Extra wide foil
Large roasting tin

Method
1. Pre heat the oven to 220°C, 450°F, gas mark 6.
2. Loosen the skin of the turkey with your hands and pack the neck end with the stuffing mix, pressing it in gently but firmly to make a rounded shaped end. Tuck the neck flap under the bird and secure with a cocktail stick.
3. Line a roasting tin with 2 sheets of foil, one laid lengthways and one widthways and both large enough to go round the bird loosely. Lay the bird on its back in the tin.
4. Rub the turkey generously all over with the softened butter, season with the salt and pepper and lay the bacon rashers over the breast making sure that they overlap.
5. Make a tent with the foil by bringing the sides of the foil up and folding together at the top, not too tight so that there is an air space around the bird.
6. Place in the pre-heated oven and cook for 30 minutes. Reduce the heat to 160°C, 325°F, gas mark 3 and cook for a further 2 ½ - 3 hours. Adjust the cooking time proportionally if a larger bird is used i.e. an extra 20 minutes per extra 450g (1lb).
7. Finish off by unwrapping the foil from the bird and tucking it into the tin in order to crisp the skin and bacon.
8. Remove onto a large serving plate and allow to stand for about 10 minutes before carving.

Hazards
Bacteria from hands and raw meat.

Critical Control Points
Wash hands thoroughly before starting especially nails and fingertips.
Wash hands after handling the raw meat, before moving on to another part of the method.

Step 6
Ensure thorough cooking by testing by piercing as deep as possible with a knife. The juices which run out should be clear and contain no traces of blood. The exposed meat should not appear bright pink at any depth. If in any doubt continue to cook and test again.

After carving
Ensure any unused meat and or stuffing is covered and refrigerated as soon as it has cooled to room temperature (maximum 90 minutes). Re-serve either cold or reheated very hot.

Use within - 2 days

Baked Sugar Glazed Boned Gammon

Ingredients - Serves 12

Small joint of boned gammon
approx. 2.25Kg (5 lbs)
1 tablespoon (15ml) mustard

1 heaped tablespoon (25g)
Demerara sugar
12 whole cloves

Cooking
Roasting tin, wide baking foil

Method
1. Either, soak the gammon joint in a large bowl of water overnight or place in a large saucepan, cover with cold water and bring to the boil. Discard the water and drain the joint on kitchen paper.
2. Pre heat the oven to 160°C, 325°F, gas mark 3.
3. Line the roasting tin with two sheets of foil, one widthways, one lengthways.
4. Place the gammon in the centre of the tin and bring one piece of foil up and over the top of the joint, folding over the top to leave an airspace. Seal the gammon securely using the other piece of foil.
5. Place in the oven and bake for 20 minutes per pound (45 minutes per Kg).
6. 30 minutes before the end of the cooking time, remove the gammon from the oven and increase the temperature to 220°C, 450°F gas mark 6.
7. Open the foil and drain off the juices. Peel off the skin and score the fat with criss-cross cuts.
8. Place a clove in each diamond shape and cover the fat with the mustard, spreading evenly with a palette or round bladed knife.
9. Sprinkle the sugar all over and press well in with your hands.
10. Return to the oven for 30 minutes or until golden brown and crisp.

Hazards

Bacteria on hands.
Cross contamination from raw meat to cooked meat, hands, utensils and surfaces.

Critical Control Points

Step 5, 10

Ensure gammon is the paler 'cooked' pink throughout and is steaming when pierced with a knife. Return to oven for further cooking if any part is not.

Use within - 5 days

Courgette Terrine

Ingredients

1kg (2lb 2oz) of courgettes
55g (2oz) butter
4 eggs
300ml (½ pint) fromage frais

2 tablespoons finely chopped
parsley and chives
Salt and pepper to season

Cooking
1.5 litre (2 ½ pint) loaf tin plus larger oven dish for the bain marie

Method
1. Grate courgettes and place in a sieve.
2. Sprinkle with salt, shake and leave for 1 hour.
3. Rinse gently in cold water and shake off excess moisture.
4. Melt most of butter in a saucepan, add the courgettes and cook gently for 10 minutes, stirring occasionally.
5. Allow to cool.
6. Pre heat oven to 180°C, 350°F, gas mark 4.
7. Use remaining butter to grease a cake or loaf tin (1.5 litres, 2 ½ pints).
8. Place the eggs in a bowl and mix lightly, mix in the fromage frais.
9. Add courgettes and herbs and season to taste with salt and pepper. Stir well to mix thoroughly.
10. Turn out mixture into tin, cover with foil and place in the oven inside a larger dish half filled with water (a bain marie).
11. Cook for 1 hour 15 minutes or until it is set.
12. Allow to cool in the tin.
13. Turn out and decorate with fresh herbs.

Hazards

Bacteria from eggs and fromage frais.

Critical Control Points

Step 11

Cook until completely set throughout. Check the middle isn't still runny by piercing with a knife and checking that no mixture sticks to it when it is withdrawn.

Use within – 5 days

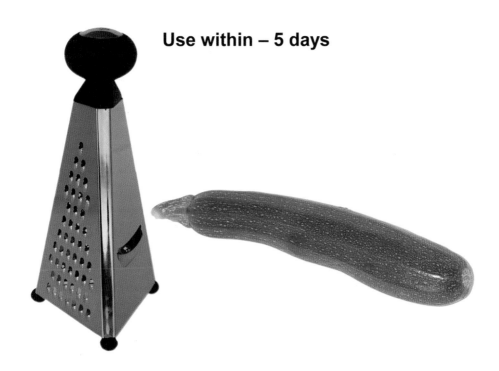

Unstuffed Roast Goose

Ingredients

Medium goose (approx 6.75Kg (15lbs))

Salt and pepper to taste

Cooking
Large roasting tin and rack

Method
1. Preheat the oven to 200°C, 400°F, gas mark 5.
2. Remove the liver and giblets if not already done and cut off the neck and loose fat and trim off the wing tips.
3. So that the fat can be released during roasting score the skin by making a cross hatch pattern of cuts on the breast at approx. 1cm intervals. Also score the legs but in one direction only. Be careful to only cut through the skin and not the meat as well.
4. Season the inside cavity and the outside with salt and pepper to taste.
5. Put the goose, breast side down on the rack in the roasting tin and place in the oven for 30 minutes.
6. Baste using the melted fat from the pan and lower the oven temperature to 180°C, 350°F, gas mark 4.
7. Cook for a further hour then remove the tin from the oven and turn the bird over so that it is now breast side up.
8. Pour off the hot fat from the tin into a heat proof container and allow to cool.
9. Replace the tin in the oven and cook for a further hour or until the juices run clear, basting approximately every 20 minutes.
10. Remove from the oven onto a large serving plate and allow to stand for at least 20 minutes before carving to allow the meat to reabsorb the juices.

Hazards
Bacteria from hands and raw goose.

Critical Control Points
Wash hands between handling of raw meat and other jobs.
Step 9
Ensure goose is cooked through out and juices run clear when a knife is inserted into the meat after cooking.
Wash all utensils in very hot water after use.

Use within - 2 days

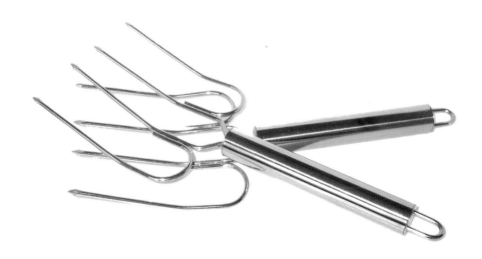

Honey Roast Pheasant

Ingredients

1Kg (2.2 lb) approx pheasant
4 tablespoons (60ml) lemon juice
Honey

Salt, black pepper, garlic powder,
tarragon and thyme to taste

Cooking
Small roasting tin

Method
1. Preheat the oven to 180°C, 350°F, gas mark 4.
2. Place the pheasant in the tin and pour over the lemon juice.
3. Spread honey generously over the whole bird.
4. Season the cavity with the salt, pepper, garlic powder, tarragon and thyme to taste and lightly sprinkle the outside.
5. Place into the bottom of the oven and roast until the juices run clear when pricked. Check after one hour of cooking. Be careful not to overcook as pheasant has very little fat and can easily become dry.

Hazards
Bacteria from hands and raw pheasant.

Critical Control Points
Wash hands between handling of raw meat and other jobs.
Step 5
Ensure pheasant is cooked through out and juices run clear when a knife is inserted into the meat after cooking.
Wash all utensils in very hot water after use.

Use within - 2 days

Traditional Christmas Pudding

Ingredients

115g (4oz) plain flour
Pinch of salt
1 teaspoon ground mixed spice
½ teaspoon ground cinnamon
¼ teaspoon grated nutmeg
225g (8oz) white breadcrumbs
350g (12oz) soft brown sugar
55g (2oz) flaked almonds
225g (8oz) raisons
225g (8oz) sultanas

115g (4oz) ready to eat dried
apricots
115g (4oz) chopped mixed peel
Finely grated rind and the juice
squeezed from one lemon
2 tablespoons (30ml) black treacle
3 eggs
300ml (½ pint) milk
2 tablespoons (30ml) rum
225g (8oz) suet
1 dessert apple

Cooking

Two, 1 litre (2 pint) greased pudding basins, greaseproof paper and string

Method

1. Sieve the flour, salt and spices into a large mixing bowl.
2. Add the suet, dried fruits and grated lemon rind and grate in the apple, stir well to mix thoroughly.
3. Heat the treacle gently in a saucepan over a low heat until warm and runny then pour into the bowl of dry ingredients.
4. In a separate bowl, mix the eggs, milk, rum and lemon juice.
5. Add the liquid into the other mixed ingredients, stirring well.
6. Spoon the mixture into the pudding basins until just below the rim.
7. Cut double layers of greaseproof paper by using the circumference of the top of the basin as a guide and allowing for the paper to come about half way down the side of the basin. Place two layers over the top of each filled basin bring down the sides and secure by tying with string.
8. Steam in a steamer or in a large pan of boiling water (The water level must not rise above the top of the basin whilst steaming). Top up water level regularly to make sure that the pan does not boil dry. Each pudding will take 8 hours to steam.
9. Allow to cool and then store in an airtight container.
10. To reheat, steam as before for a further 1½ hours.

Hazards
Bacteria in eggs.

Critical Control Points
Step 7, 10
Steam (or reheat) the pudding until it is completely set and too hot to eat in the centre.

Use within - 3 months

Baked Soured Cream Cheese Cake

Ingredients - Serves 10

55g (2oz) butter, melted
115g (4oz) digestive biscuits, crushed
¼ teaspoon ground cinnamon
450g (1lb) cream cheese, softened
145g (5oz) sugar
3 eggs, beaten

Grated rind of 1 lemon
2 tablespoons (30ml) lemon juice
1½ teaspoons vanilla essence
300ml (½ pint) soured cream (if unavailable substitute fresh cream but add 4 drops of lemon juice).
Grated lemon and lime rind to decorate

Cooking
Loose bottom cake tin

Method
1.   Mix together the melted butter, biscuit crumbs and cinnamon.
2.   Press the mixture into a loose bottom cake tin to form the base.
3.   Cook at 180°C, 350°F, gas mark 4 for 10 minutes.
4.   Cream together the cheese and 115g (4oz) of the sugar and gradually beat in the eggs.
5.   Stir in the lemon rind, juice and vanilla essence.
6.   Pour the mixture onto the biscuit crumb base and bake at the same temperature as the base for 1 hour or until the centre is firm to touch.
7.   Remove from the oven and increase the temperature to 230°C, 450°F, gas mark 8.
8.   Mix together the remaining sugar and soured cream and spread over the cheesecake. Bake for 10 minutes or until set.
9.   Remove from the oven and allow to cool in the tin.
10. Remove from the tin and chill until ready to serve, decorate with lemon and lime rind.

Hazards
Bacteria in cheese, cream and raw eggs.

Critical Control Points
Step 6, 8
Ensure that the cheesecake is hot through to the middle.

Use within – 24 hours

Traditional Sherry Trifle

Ingredients - Serves 6

5 trifle sponges
Raspberry jam
225g (8oz) frozen raspberries
50ml (2fl oz) sherry
2 small bananas, peeled and sliced

For the custard
300ml (½ pint) single cream
3 egg yolks
25g (1oz) caster sugar
1 level teaspoon cornflour

To decorate
300ml (½ pint) double cream
55g (2oz) flaked almond, lightly toasted

Method

1. Break sponges into pieces (5cm / 2 inches) and spread with jam.
2. Place in the bottom of a large bowl with the raspberries and sherry and stir well to allow the sherry to be soaked up.
3. Heat the single cream gently in a saucepan.
4. In a small bowl blend the egg yolks, sugar and cornflour together.
5. Pour the hot cream over the mixture, stirring constantly.
6. Return to the saucepan and stir over a very low heat until thick. Allow to cool.
7. Slice the bananas, place in bowl evenly over the raspberry and sponge mixture and pour over the custard evenly.
8. Whip the double cream and spread gently on top of the custard. Decorate with flaked almonds.
9. Cover and chill before serving.

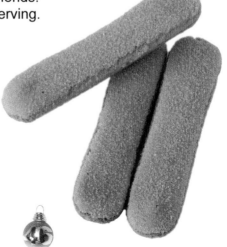

Hazards
Bacteria from hands and eggs.
Sensitivity to nuts (omit or choose a different decoration if unsure).

Critical Control Points
Before starting wash hands thoroughly, especially nails and finger tips.

Step 6
Heat the custard mix until it is hot and consistently thickened throughout.
Step 9
Cool to below 10°C within 90 minutes.

Use within – 2 days

Chocolate Orange Trifle

Ingredients - Serves 4

1 chocolate swiss roll
1 can mandarin orange segments
2 tablespoons orange juice or brandy
150ml (5fl oz) fresh double cream

1 tablespoon (15ml) fresh milk
2 tablespoons (30g) sifted icing sugar
55g (2oz) plain chocolate, grated, for decoration

Method

1. Cut swiss roll into 10 slices and arrange evenly In the base of a large attractive bowl.
2. Pour in the oranges and juice from the tin and either the brandy or orange juice as desired, ensuring the orange segments are evenly spread.
3. Whip the cream and milk together until stiff and then stir in the sugar.
4. Pour the mixture over the oranges, spreading evenly and chill in the fridge.
5. Just before serving sprinkle with the grated chocolate.

Hazards

Bacteria in the cream and milk.

Critical Control Points

Step 3
Use only pasteurised or UHT milk or cream and ensure they are refrigerated before use.
Steps 4, 5
Ensure the trifle is covered and refrigerated below 10°C until served.

Use within - 24 hours

Chocolate Bread Pudding

Ingredients

250ml milk
250ml single cream
115g (4oz) sugar
115g (4oz) cooking chocolate

4 eggs
1 teaspoon (5ml) vanilla essence
225g (8oz) white bread, cubed into
1cm (½ Inch) cubes

Cooking
Oven proof glass baking dish

Method

1. Preheat oven to 180°C, 350°F gas mark 4.
2. Combine the milk, cream and sugar in a large heavy saucepan over a medium high heat and stir until the sugar dissolves and the just mixture comes to the boil.
3. Remove from the heat and add the chocolate, stirring until smooth.
4. Beat the eggs together in a large bowl and blend in the vanilla essence.
5. Gradually add the chocolate mixture, whisking gently.
6. Add the bread cubes and leave to stand for a minimum 30 minutes so some of the custard is absorbed, stirring occasionally.
7. Transfer to glass baking dish and cover with foil.
8. Bake until it is set in the centre which will take about 1 hour.
9. Serve while still warm with cream or custard.

Hazards
Bacteria in raw eggs.

Critical Control Points
Step 8
Ensure cooked throughout and set in the centre.

Use within - 2 days

Figgy Pudding

Ingredients

225g (8oz) soft dried figs
250g (10oz) soft white bread crumbs
115g (4oz) chopped almonds and / or walnuts
225g (8oz) light brown sugar

85g (3oz) candied peel
3 tablespoons (45ml) melted butter
4 eggs, beaten
½ teaspoon cinnamon
½ teaspoon nutmeg
1 teaspoon (15ml) dark rum

Cooking
1 litre (2 pint) pudding basin, lightly greased
Foil or grease proof paper

Method
1. Chop the figs and mix with the breadcrumbs in a large mixing bowl.
2. Mix in all the other dry ingredients.
3. Add the beaten egg, melted butter and the rum and mix thoroughly.
4. Put the mixture into a greased pudding bowl and cover with foil or grease-proof paper and string and steam for 2 ½ hours.
5. Serve hot with cream, custard or brandy butter.

Hazards
Bacteria in raw eggs.
Mould and foreign bodies in nuts.

Critical Control Points
Step 4
Ensure fully cooked and set in the centre.
Re-heat thoroughly by steaming for 1 hour or microwave for 3 - 4 minutes if stored.

Use within - 3 months

Sausage Rolls

Ingredients - Makes 24

Flaky pastry
225g (8oz) plain flour
175g (6oz) butter or margarine
Pinch of salt
Cold water for mixing
(Or use ready bought frozen and
follow directions for use)

Filling
One medium sized onion finely
chopped
450g (1lb) pork sausage meat
1 teaspoon dried sage
Finishing
1 egg, beaten

Cooking
2 baking sheets, lightly greased

Method
1. Wrap butter or margarine (fat) in foil and place in freezer for 30 minutes.
2. Meanwhile, sieve flour and salt together into a mixing bowl.
3. Remove fat and grate into the bowl of flour using largest holes on grater.
4. Mix with a palette or other flat bladed knife, add water gradually mixing well until a dough is formed. Place in a polythene bag and chill in the fridge for 30 minutes.
5. Meanwhile mix the sausage meat, onion and sage together in a bowl.
6. Roll out pastry using a rolling pin onto a floured surface to form an oblong shape that is as thin as possible without breaking up.
7. Take a handful of filling and gently roll out into a sausage shape over the pastry to the same length as the longest side, starting at the nearest edge. (If it is too sticky sprinkle on a little flour).
8. Turn the pastry over the roll of filling one and a half turns and seal the edge with the beaten egg by brushing lightly using a pastry brush. Cut off the excess pastry and repeat with another handful of sausage meat.
9. Cut the completed sausage rolls into 5cm (2 inch) lengths and score three lines into the top of each one with a knife. Glaze the top with beaten egg.
10. Place onto a baking sheet and bake in the oven at 220°C, 450°F, gas mark 7 for 20-25 minutes or until golden brown.
11. Allow to cool slightly before serving.
12. Place in fridge or freeze if not used immediately.

Hazards
Bacteria from hands, meat, surfaces, and egg.
Recontamination after cooking.

Critical Control Points
Wash hands thoroughly before and after handling raw sausage meat.

Step 10
Ensure cooking is sufficient to raise the temperature of the meat so it is too hot to handle - it should burn if bitten into when first out of the oven!
Step 11
Store below 10°C and if reheated before serving, ensure they are 'piping hot'. Take especial care if cooking from frozen to ensure that the middle of the meat is too hot to touch.

General advice
Keep all cooked ingredients away from uncooked.
If you have to use the same surfaces or utensils for cooked and uncooked ingredients then they should be thoroughly cleaned / scalded / wiped with a sanitiser both before and after each change of use.

Use within - 2 days

Hazelnut Cakes

Ingredients - Makes 12

225g (8oz) self raising flour
115g (4oz) castor sugar
85g (3oz) butter or margarine

1 large egg, beaten
85g (3oz) chopped hazelnuts
3 drops vanilla essence

Cooking
Paper cases or a patty tin

Method
1.	Cream together the sugar and butter in a large mixing bowl.
2.	Add the beaten egg, vanilla essence, flour and nuts and mix thoroughly.
3.	Half fill paper cake cases with the mixture and place on a baking tray or use a well greased patty tin.
4.	Bake in oven at 180°C, 350°F, gas mark 4 for about 20 minutes until golden.
5.	Cool and store in an airtight container until required.

Hazards
Bacteria in egg.
Mould and bacteria on nuts.

Critical Control Points
Step 4
Ensure thorough cooking by piercing with a knife, cakes that are in different positions on the tray. When cooked the knife should be clear when withdrawn, without any cake mix sticking to it

Use within - 5 days

Rich Shortbread

Ingredients - Makes 8

115g (4oz) softened butter
55g (2oz) caster sugar
145g (5oz) plain flour

25g (1oz) semolina
Extra castor sugar for dredging

Cooking
Greased 18cm (7 inch) sandwich tin

Method
1. Cream butter and sugar together in a mixing bowl until light and fluffy.
2. Gradually sieve and stir flour into bowl with a fork, then gradually add the semolina, also stirring with a fork.
3. Press the mixture evenly into the tin.
4. Prick all over with fork.
5. Bake in the oven at 160°C, 325°F, gas mark 3 for 40 minutes or until pale golden in colour.
6. Leave in the tin for 5 minutes then cut into eight triangles and sprinkle lightly with castor sugar.
7. When cold remove from tin and store in an airtight container.

Hazards
Bacteria on hands.

Critical Control Points
Step 3
Wash hands thoroughly.
Step 5
Ensure the biscuit is too hot too handle when it is removed from the oven.

Use within - 2 weeks

Chocolate Truffles

225g (8oz) good quality plain chocolate (semi-sweet) broken into small pieces
240ml (8fl oz) double cream
40g (1 ½ oz) unsalted butter
3 tablespoons (45ml) brandy, rum or other spirit to flavour if desired

Coatings –
Choose from chocolate vermicelli, cocoa powder, finely chopped nuts or icing sugar.

Cooking
Baking sheet, non stick paper, paper cases

Method
1. Bring the cream just to the boil in a saucepan.
2. Remove from the heat and add the broken chocolate, stirring until melted.
3. Stir in the butter until melted completely.
4. Add the spirit, ensuring the mixture is well mixed.
5. Pour the mixture into a bowl and leave to cool.
6. When cool refrigerate for at least four hours but preferably overnight.
7. Line a baking sheet with non stick paper and using a melon ball maker or teaspoon make balls from the chilled chocolate mixture and place each on the sheet.
8. Place a little of the chosen coating on a plate or plates (separate) and carefully roll each truffle until evenly coated.
9. Keep in the fridge until required.
10. Serve in individual paper cases or place on a dish or plate.

Hazards
Bacteria in cream.
Recontamination of the cream rich mixture after boiling.
Hypersensitivity to nuts in some people, if in doubt omit.
Hypersensitivity to dairy product in some people.

Critical Control Points
Step 1
Ensure cream just boils to kill any bacteria present.
Step 8
Wash hands thoroughly before handling the truffles.
Step 9, 10
Ensure storage is below 5°C until close to serving

Use within – 10 days if refrigerated
(or if frozen for up to 8 weeks)

Mince Pies

Ingredients - Makes 12

For the pastry
225g (8oz) plain flour
145g (5oz) butter
¼ teaspoon salt
4-5 tablespoons (60–75ml) cold water

For the pies
450g (1lb) jar of ready bought mincemeat or use home made
1 egg, beaten, for glazing
Icing sugar for dredging

Cooking
12 hole deep patty tin, greased

Method
1. Sieve the flour and salt into a large mixing bowl.
2. Rub in the butter with the fingertips until the mixture resembles fine breadcrumbs.
3. Sprinkle water over the crumbs carefully and mix to a stiff paste. Be careful not to overwet. Place the lump of mixture into a polythene bag and chill in the fridge for 30 minutes.
4. Turn out onto a floured surface and knead until smooth and crack free.
5. Roll out the pastry onto a floured surface as thin as possible without it tearing.
6. Cut 12 rounds with a small cutter for the lids and 12 rounds with a slightly bigger cutter for the bases.
7. Place the bases in the greased patty tin and place a heaped teaspoonful of mincemeat in each.
8. Moisten the edges of the bases with water using a pastry brush and place the lids on top, firming down gently around the edges with fingertips.
9. Brush tops with beaten egg to glaze, with a pastry brush.
10. Bake at 220°C, 450°F, gas mark 7 for 20 to 25 minutes or until golden brown.
11. Remove from tin and dredge with icing sugar.

Hazards
Bacteria in egg and mincemeat and on hands.

Critical Control Points
Wash hands thoroughly, especially nails and fingertips.
Step 10
Ensure pies are cooked through and the mincemeat is too hot to taste.
Keep covered until cool and store in an airtight container until required.

Use within - 10 days

Weights and Measures

Dry weights

Metric	Imperial
15g	½oz
25g	1oz
55g	2oz
85g	3oz
115g	4oz (¼lb)
145g	5oz
175g	6oz
200g	7oz
225g	8oz (½lb)
350g	12oz (¾ lb)
450g	16oz (1lb)
1000g (1kg)	2lb 2oz

Liquid Measures

Metric	Imperial
5ml	1 Teaspoon
15ml	1 Table Spoon
50ml	2floz
150ml	5floz (¼ pint)
300ml	10floz (½ pint)
450ml	15floz (¾ pint)
600ml	20floz (1 pint)
1000ml (Litre)	1¾ pints

Temperatures

Celsius (°C)	Fahrenheit (°F)	Gas Mark
120	250	1
150	300	2
160	325	3
180	350	4
200	400	5
220	450	6
240	500	7

All figures are rounded to make measuring easier, so please stick to either metric or imperial measures when following a recipe.

Notes

Notes

Notes

Notes

Notes